Activating God's Power

in **Delina**

by Michelle Leslie

Activating God's Power

ISBN: 978-1-63594-368-9

DEDICATION

For Delina

Activating God's Power

CONTENTS

Activating God's Power

ACKNOWLEDGMENTS

Thank you to God, my family, mentors, friends, and neighbors for all your love and support as God prepared me to put this book together.

May the Lord bless you and keep you, the Lord make His face shine upon you and be gracious to you; the Lord turn His face toward you and give you peace.

Numbers 6:24

Activating God's Power

ACTIVATING GOD'S POWER
IN YOUR LIFE
AND IN OTHERS'

Sometimes we don't know what or how to pray, but we are in need of God's power in our lives. When we pray God's word we can never pray outside God's will for our lives or the lives of others. When we meditate on the word and speak it we are activating God's power. God's word brings life and creates a spiritual mindset that changes us and the world around us (Romans 12:2).

There are many great books on overcoming addiction, having a successful marriage, being effective in ministry, overcoming anxiety, or being a great parent. I challenge you that the solution to all of the above is God's word. There is no formula to solve these issues, but the word of God's word is alive (Hebrews 4:12) and can empower you to do and be what God is calling you or others to do and be in any circumstance. It transforms the heart and the mind. The word of God brings clarity and strength.

However different from person to person, we all have challenging circumstances and personal weaknesses to overcome. God tells us in the book of Ephesians to use His word (the sword of the Spirit) to fight these battles. We will overcome and will be transformed when we access God's power available in His word. Jesus says in John 8:31-32, "If you abide in my word, you are truly my disciples, and you will know the truth, and the truth will set you free."

God's power is available to each one of us. Activate His power in your life and in the lives of those around you. Speak it, personalize it, and let the power of God transform your life and circumstances.

Anxiety

Delina is strong and courageous. Delina is not afraid or terrified because the Lord her God goes with her; He will never leave her nor forsake Delina.

Deuteronomy 31:6

The Lord goes before Delina and is with her; He will never leave Delina or forsake her. Delina is not afraid or discouraged.

Deuteronomy 31:8

Delina fears no evil because the Lord is with her; God's word and Spirit comfort Delina.

Psalm 23:4

Delina casts her burdens on the Lord, and He sustains her; He will never permit the righteous to be moved.

Psalm 55:22

Anxiety

"Delina comes to me when she labors and is heavy laden, and I give her rest. Delina takes my yoke upon her, and learns from me, for I am gentle and lowly in heart, and she finds rest for her soul. For my yoke is easy, and my burden is light."

Matthew 11:28-30

Peace I leave with Delina; my peace I give to her. Not as the world gives do I give to Delina. Delina lets not her heart be troubled, neither does she let her heart be afraid.

John 14:27

Delina rejoices in the Lord always and lets her gentleness be evident to all. The Lord is near to Delina so she is not anxious about anything, but in every situation, by prayer and petition, with thanksgiving, she presents her requests to God. And the peace of God, which transcends all understanding, guards Delina's heart and mind in Christ Jesus.

Philippians 4:4-7

Anxiety

Delina casts all her anxiety on Him because He cares for Delina.

1 Peter 5:7

When Delina lies down, she will not be afraid; when Delina lies down, her sleep will be sweet. Delina has no fear of sudden disaster or of the ruin that overtakes the wicked, for the Lord is at her side and will keep her foot from being snared.

Proverbs 3:24-26

Blessing & Favor

May the Lord bless and keep Delina; the Lord make His face to shine on Delina and be gracious to her; the Lord turn His face toward Delina and give her peace.

Numbers 6:24-26

As Delina listens to these commands of the Lord and is careful to obey them, the Lord will make Delina the head and not the tail, and Delina will always be at the top and never at the bottom.

Deuteronomy 28:13

"Oh, that You would bless Delina indeed, and enlarge Delina's territory. May Your hand be with Delina, and keep Delina from evil, that it may not cause her pain."

1 Chronicles 4:10

Blessing & Favor

You gave Delina life and showed her kindness, and in your providence You watched over her spirit.

Job 10:12

May the favor of the Lord our God rest on Delina; and establish the work of Delina's hands—yes, establish the work of Delina's hands.

Psalm 90:17

For You bless the righteous, O Lord; you cover Delina with favor as with a shield.

Psalm 5:12

You prepare a table before Delina in the presence of her enemies; you anoint her head with oil; Delina's cup overflows. Surely goodness and mercy shall follow Delina all the days of her life, and she shall dwell in the house of the Lord forever.

Psalm 23:5-6

Blessing & Favor

Delina is like a tree planted by streams of water that yields its fruit in its season, and its leaf does not wither. In all that Delina does, she prospers.

Psalm 1:3

Delina is blessed because she fears the Lord; she greatly delights in His commandments. Delina's descendants will be mighty on earth; the generation of the upright will be blessed.

Psalm 112:1-2

Blessing & Favor

For the Lord God is Delina's sun and shield; the Lord bestows favor and honor on Delina; no good thing does He withhold from Delina whose walk is blameless.

Psalm 84:11

"For I will pour water on Delina when she is thirsty, and floods on the dry ground; I will pour My Spirit on Delina's descendants, and My blessing on Delina's offspring; they will spring up among the grass like willows by the watercourses. One will say, 'I am the Lord's'; another will call himself by the name of Jacob; another will write with his hand, 'The Lord's,' and name himself by the name of Israel."

Isaiah 44:3-5

"For I know the plans I have for Delina," declares the Lord, "plans to prosper Delina and not to harm her, plans to give Delina hope and a future."

Jeremiah 29:11

Blessing & Favor

Thank you Lord that it will come to pass that You will pour out Your Spirit on Delina; Delina shall prophesy, dream dreams, and see visions.

Joel 2:28

The heart of Delina is like good soil; she hears the word, accepts it, and produces a crop—some hundred times that which she has sown.

Mark 4:20

He who supplies seed to the sower and bread for food will supply and multiply Delina's seed for sowing and increase the harvest of her righteousness.

2 Corinthians 9:10

Calling

The Lord makes firm the steps of Delina who delights in Him.

Psalm 37:23

Your word is a lamp to Delina's feet and a light to Delina's path.

Psalm 119:105

Delina trusts in the Lord with all of her heart. Delina leans not on her own understanding; in all Delina's ways she acknowledges God and God directs Delina's path.

Proverbs 3:5-6

In her heart Delina plans her course, but the Lord establishes Delina's steps.

Proverbs 16:9

Calling

"For I know the plans I have for you Delina," declares the Lord, "plans for you to prosper and not to harm you, to give you a future and a hope. Then Delina will call upon me and come and pray to me, and I will hear her. Delina will seek me and find me, when Delina seeks me with all of her heart."

Jeremiah 29:11-13

God's gifts and His call on Delina are irrevocable.

Romans 11:29

May the eyes of Delina's heart be enlightened, that she may know what is the hope to which He has called her, what are the riches of His glorious inheritance in the saints.

Ephesians 1:18

Delina lives a life worthy of the calling she has received.

Ephesians 4:1

Calling

He who began a good work in Delina will be faithful to complete it.

Philippians 1:6

For it is God who works in Delina to will and to act in order to fulfill His good purpose.

Philippians 2:13

With this in mind, we constantly pray for Delina, that our God may make Delina worthy of His calling, and that by His power He may bring to fruition Delina's every desire for goodness and deed prompted by faith.

2 Thessalonians 1:11

He has saved Delina and called her to a holy life—not because of anything she has done but because of His own purpose and grace.

2 Timothy 1:9

Calling

When Delina lacks wisdom, she asks God, who gives generously to all without reproach, and it is given to her.

James 1:5

Delina is diligent to confirm her calling and election. As Delina practices these qualities she will never fall.

2 Peter 1:10

Character

Delina's integrity and uprightness protect her, because Delina's hope, Lord, is in you.

Psalm 25:21

Delina does not walk in the counsel of the ungodly or stand in the path of sinners or sit in the seat of scoffers. But Delina delights herself in the law of the Lord and Delina meditates on His law day and night. Delina is like a tree planted by the rivers of water, which yields its fruit in season and whose leaf will not wither, and whatever she does she prospers.

Psalm 1:1-3

Delina walks with integrity; her children are blessed after her.

Proverbs 20:7

Delina is concerned about the Lord's affairs; her aim is to be devoted to the Lord in both body and spirit.

1 Corinthians 7:34

Character

Delina is very careful how she lives—not as unwise but wise, making the most of every opportunity.

Ephesians 5:15-16

God, as one of Your chosen people, holy and dearly loved, help Delina to clothe herself with compassion, kindness, humility, gentleness, and patience.

Colossians 3:12

Delina shows proper respect to everyone. Delina loves the family of believers, fears God, and honors the emperor.

1 Peter 2:17

Direction

Your word is a lamp to Delina's feet and a light to Delina's path.

Psalm 119:105

He refreshes Delina's soul. He guides Delina along the right paths for His name's sake.

Psalm 23:3

"I will instruct Delina and teach her in the way she should go; I will counsel Delina with my eye upon her."

Psalm 32:8

The Lord's angels keep charge over Delina to guard her in all her ways.

Psalm 91:11

The Lord makes firm the steps of Delina who delights in Him.

Psalm 37:23

Direction

In her heart Delina plans her course, but the Lord establishes Delina's steps.

Proverbs 16:9

Delina trusts in the Lord with all of her heart. Delina leans not on her own understanding; in all Delina's ways she acknowledges God and God directs Delina's path.

Proverbs 3:5-6

The Lord will guide Delina always; He will satisfy Delina's needs in a sun-scorched land and will strengthen Delina's frame. Delina will be like a well-watered garden, like a spring whose waters never fail.

Isaiah 58:11

Discernment

Delina, do not forget my teaching, but let your heart keep my commandments, for the length of days and years of life and peace they will add to you. Let not steadfast love and faithfulness forsake you, Delina; bind them around your neck; write them on the tablet of your heart. So you will find favor and good success in the sight of God and man. Trust in the Lord with all of your heart, and do not lean on your own understanding.

Proverbs 3:1-5

Delina does follow the Good Shepherd and Delina knows His voice, and the voice of a stranger Delina will not follow.

John 10:4-5

Delina does not conform to the pattern of this world, but she is transformed by the renewing of her mind. Delina is able to test and approve what God's will is— His good, pleasing and perfect will.

Romans 12:2

Discernment

And this is my prayer: that Delina's love may abound more and more in knowledge and depth of insight, so that Delina may be able to discern what is best and may be pure and blameless for the day of Christ.

Philippians 1:9-10

Delina tests everything. Delina holds on to what is good. Delina avoids every kind of evil.

1 Thessalonians 5:21-22

But solid food is for the mature. By constant use Delina has trained herself to distinguish good from evil.

Hebrews 5:14

Discipline

Delina does not let the book of the Law depart from her mouth. Delina meditates on it day and night. Delina is careful to do everything written in it, so she will be prosperous and successful.

Joshua 1:8

Delina hides God's word in her heart so she is careful to not sin against Him.

Psalm 119:11

Blessed is Delina whom You discipline, O Lord, and You teach Delina out of Your law, to give Delina rest from days of trouble. For the Lord will not forsake Delina; He will not abandon Delina's heritage.

Psalm 94:12-14

Discipline

Delina does not run aimlessly; she does not fight like a boxer beating the air. But Delina disciplines her body and keeps it under control.

1 Corinthians 9:26-28

Delina lives by the Spirit, and does not gratify the desires of sinful nature.

Galatians 5:16

Delina does not let the sun go down on her anger, and she does not give the devil an opportunity.

Ephesians 4:26

Delina does not regard lightly the discipline of the Lord, nor is she weary when reproved by Him. For the Lord disciplines the one He loves, and chastises every child whom He receives.

Hebrews 12:5-6

Encouragement

May the God who gives endurance and encouragement give Delina a spirit of unity with others as she follows Christ Jesus.

Romans 15:5

Delina has encouragement from being united with Christ. Delina has comfort from His love, fellowship with the Spirit, His tenderness and compassion. Delina's joy is complete because she is like-minded with Christ and has the same love and is one with Christ in spirit and purpose. Delina does nothing out of selfish ambition or vain conceit, but in humility, Delina considers others better than herself and looks to the interests of others. Delina's attitude is the same as that of Christ Jesus.

Philippians 2

Encouragement

Delina is encouraged in heart and united in love. Delina has the full riches and complete understanding of the mysteries of God, namely Christ, in whom are hidden all the treasures of wisdom and understanding.

Colossians 2

Faith

Therefore I tell you, whatever Delina asks for in prayer, she believes that she has received it, and it will be hers.

Mark 11:24

Faith comes from hearing, and hearing through the word of God. Delina's faith increases every time she hears or reads the word of God.

Romans 10:17

For it is with Delina's heart that she believes and is justified, and it is with her mouth that Delina professes her faith and is saved.

Romans 10:10

Faith

Delina does not lose heart. Though outwardly she is wasting away, yet inwardly Delina is being renewed day by day, for Delina's light and momentary troubles are achieving for her an eternal glory that far outweighs them all. So Delina fixes her eyes not on what is seen, but what is unseen, since what is seen is temporary, but what is unseen is eternal.

2 Corinthians 4:16-18

Delina has been crucified with Christ. Delina no longer lives, but Christ lives in her. The life Delina now lives in the body, she lives by faith in the Son of God, who loved her and gave Himself for her.

Galatians 2:20

Faith

For it is by grace Delina has been saved, through faith—
and this is not from yourselves, it is the gift of God—
not by works, so that no one can boast. For Delina is
God's handiwork, created in Christ Jesus to do good
works, which God prepared in advance for Delina to do.

Ephesians 2:8-10

Delina knows that the testing of her faith produces
perseverance.

James 1:3

Though Delina has not seen Him, she loves Him; and
even though Delina does not see Him now, she believes
in Him and is filled with an inexpressible and glorious
joy, for Delina is receiving the end result of her faith, the
salvation of her soul.

1 Peter 1:8-9

Family

Delina prayed for her child, and the Lord has granted her what she asked of Him.

1 Samuel 1:27

Delina is blessed because she fears the Lord; she greatly delights in His commandments. Delina's descendants will be mighty on earth; the generation of the upright will be blessed.

Psalm 112:1-2

Delina walks with integrity; her children are blessed after her.

Proverbs 20:7

Delina has been trained up in the way she should go; and when she is old, she will not depart from it.

Proverbs 22:6

Family

"For I will pour water on Delina when she is thirsty, and floods on the dry ground; I will pour My Spirit on Delina's descendants, and My blessing on Delina's offspring; they will spring up among the grass like willows by the watercourses. One will say, 'I am the Lord's'; another will call himself by the name of Jacob; another will write with his hand, 'The Lord's,' and name himself by the name of Israel."

Isaiah 44:3-5

Thus says the Lord: "Delina restrains her voice from weeping, and her eyes from tears; for her work shall be rewarded," says the Lord, "They shall come back from the land of the enemy. There is hope in Delina's future," says the Lord, "That your children shall come back to their own border."

Jeremiah 31:16-17

Family

———— ⌒⌒⌒ ————

Delina obeys her parents in the Lord. Delina honors her father and mother so that it may go well with her and that Delina may enjoy long life on earth.

Ephesians 6:1-3

Fear

Delina is strong and courageous. Delina is not afraid or terrified because the Lord her God goes with her; He will never leave her nor forsake Delina.

Deuteronomy 31:6

The Lord goes before Delina and is with her; He will never leave Delina or forsake her. Delina is not afraid or discouraged.

Deuteronomy 31:8

Delina fears no evil because the Lord is with her; God's word and Spirit comfort Delina.

Psalm 23:4

When Delina lies down, she will not be afraid; when Delina lies down, her sleep will be sweet. Delina has no fear of sudden disaster or of the ruin that overtakes the wicked, for the Lord is at her side and will keep her foot from being snared.

Proverbs 3:24-26

Fear

"Delina fears not, I am with her; Delina is not dismayed, for I am her God; I will strengthen Delina, I will help her, I will uphold Delina with my righteous right hand."

Isaiah 41:10

Delina rejoices in the Lord always and lets her gentleness be evident to all. The Lord is near to Delina so she is not anxious about anything, but in every situation, by prayer and petition, with thanksgiving, she presents her requests to God. And the peace of God, which transcends all understanding, guards Delina's heart and mind in Christ Jesus.

Philippians 4:4-7

Delina casts all her anxiety on Him because He cares for Delina.

1 Peter 5:7

Forgiveness

As far as the east is from the west, so far has He removed Delina's transgressions from her.

Psalm 103:12

Delina loves her enemies; she does good to those who hate her.

Luke 6:27

Delina forgives, as the Lord has forgiven her.

Colossians 3:13

"Delina's sins and lawless acts I will remember no more."

Hebrews 10:17

Freedom

Out of Delina's distress she called on the Lord; the Lord answered Delina and set her free.

Psalm 118:5

Delina will know the truth, and the truth will set Delina free.

John 8:32

So if the Son sets Delina free, Delina will be free indeed.

John 8:36

Delina is dead to sin but alive to God in Christ Jesus.

Romans 6:11

Delina has the right to do anything, but not everything is beneficial to her. Delina has the right to do anything, but she will not be mastered by anything.

1 Corinthians 6:12

Freedom

It is for freedom that Christ has set Delina free. Delina stands firm, then, and does not let herself be burdened again by a yoke of slavery.

Galatians 5:1

Delina was called to freedom. Delina does not use her freedom as an opportunity for the flesh, but through love she serves others.

Galatians 5:13

In Him and through faith Delina approaches God with freedom and confidence.

Ephesians 3:12

Delina lives as a person who is free, not using her freedom as a cover-up for evil, but living as a servant of God.

1 Peter 2:16

Grace

God's grace is sufficient for Delina, for His power is made perfect in her weakness.

2 Corinthians 12:9

He who began a good work in Delina will be faithful to complete it.

Philippians 1:6

For it is God who works in Delina to will and to act in order to fulfill His good purpose.

Philippians 2:13

Grace and peace be Delina's in abundance through the knowledge of God and of Jesus our Lord. His divine power has given Delina everything she needs for a godly life through our knowledge of Him who called her by His own glory and goodness.

2 Peter 1:2-3

Healing

Delina serves the Lord her God, and He blesses her bread and her water. He will take sickness away from her.

Exodus 23:25

O Lord my God, Delina cries to You for help, and You have healed her.

Psalm 30:2

Delina blesses the Lord with all her soul, and forgets not all His benefits, who forgives all her iniquity, who heals all her diseases.

Psalm 103:2-3

He sent out His word and healed Delina, and delivered her from her destruction.

Psalm 107:20

Healing

―――――― ᘓᗛᘔ ――――――

Delina shall not die, but she shall live, and recount the deeds of the Lord.

Psalm 118:17

He heals Delina's broken heart and binds up her wounds.

Psalm 147:3

Delina is not wise in her own eyes; she fears the Lord, and turns away from evil. It is healing to her flesh and refreshment to her bones.

Proverbs 3:7-8

Delina pays attention to what I say; she turns her ear to my words. Delina does not let them escape from her sight; she keeps them within her heart. For they are life to Delina and healing to her flesh.

Proverbs 4:20-22

Healing

He was pierced for Delina's transgressions; He was crushed for her iniquities; upon Him was the chastisement that brought Delina peace, and with His wounds she is healed.

Isaiah 53:5

Then Your light will break forth like the dawn, and Delina's healing will quickly appear; then Your righteousness will go before Delina, and the glory of the Lord will be her rear guard.

Isaiah 58:8

Heal Delina, O Lord, and she shall be healed; save Delina, and she shall be saved, for You are Delina's praise.

Jeremiah 17:14

"Take heart, Delina; your faith has made you well."

Matthew 9:22

Healing

And these signs shall follow Delina, who believes; in Christ's name she shall cast out devils; she shall speak with new tongues; she shall pick up serpents; and if she drinks any deadly thing, it shall not hurt her; she shall lay hands on the sick, and they shall recover.

Mark 16:17-18

And the prayer of faith will save Delina when she is sick, and the Lord will raise her. And if she has committed sins, she will be forgiven.

James 5:15

He Himself bore Delina's sins in His body on the tree, that Delina might die to sin and live to righteousness. By His wounds Delina has been healed.

1 Peter 2:24

Delina, I pray that all may go well with you and that you may be in good health, as it goes well with your soul.

3 John 1:2

Hope

"For I know the plans I have for you Delina," declares the Lord, "plans to prosper you and not to harm you, to give you a future and a hope. Then Delina will call upon me and come and pray to me, and I will hear her. Delina will seek me and find me, when Delina seeks me with all of her heart."

Jeremiah 29:11-13

Delina hopes in the Lord and the Lord renews her strength. Delina will soar on wings like an eagle. Delina will run and not grow weary. Delina will walk and not be faint.

Isaiah 40:31

Delina knows that in all things God works for the good of those who love Him, and have been called according to His purpose.

Romans 8:28

Hope

May the God of hope fill Delina with all joy and peace in believing, so that by the power of the Holy Spirit Delina may abound in hope.

Romans 15:13

Delina is joyful in hope, patient in affliction, faithful in prayer.

Romans 12:12

Delina rejoices in her sufferings, knowing that suffering produces endurance, and endurance produces character, and character produces hope, and hope does not put Delina to shame, because God's love has been poured into her heart through the Holy Spirit who has been given to her.

Romans 5:3-5

Humility

Delina does not think of herself more highly than she ought, but rather she thinks of herself with sober judgment, in accordance with the faith God has distributed to her.

Romans 12:3

Delina does nothing out of selfish ambition or vain conceit, but in humility she doesn't consider herself better than others. Delina does not only look out for her own interests, but also the interests of others. Delina has this mindset which was also in Christ Jesus.

Philippians 2:3-5

Delina humbles herself before the Lord, and the Lord will lift Delina up.

James 4:10

Delina humbles herself under God's mighty hand, that He may lift her up in due time.

1 Peter 5:6

Identity

Before God formed Delina in the womb He knew her;
before Delina was born He set her apart.

Jeremiah 1:5

Delina is united with the Lord and is one with Him in
spirit.

1 Corinthians 6:17

Delina has been crucified with Christ. Delina no longer
lives, but Christ lives in her. The life Delina now lives in
the flesh she lives by faith in the Son of God, who loved
her and gave himself for her.

Galatians 2:20

Delina is God's workmanship, created in Christ Jesus to
do good works, which God created in advance for
Delina to do.

Ephesians 2:10

Identity

God, as one of Your chosen people, holy and dearly loved, help Delina to clothe herself with compassion, kindness, humility, gentleness, and patience.

Colossians 3:12

The Spirit of the Lord is upon Delina because He has anointed Delina to preach the good news to the poor. He has sent Delina to bind up the brokenhearted, to proclaim freedom for the captives and release from darkness for the prisoners, to proclaim the year of the Lord's favor and the day of vengeance of our God. Delina comforts those who mourn, and provides for those who grieve in Zion. Delina bestows on them a crown of beauty instead of ashes, the oil of gladness instead of mourning, and a garment of praise instead of the spirit of despair.

Isaiah 61:1-3

Joy

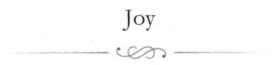

Delina does not grieve, for the joy of the Lord is Delina's strength.

Nehemiah 8:10

The Lord is Delina's strength and shield; Delina's heart trusts in Him, and He helps Delina. Delina's heart leaps for joy, and with a song Delina praises Him.

Psalm 28:7

Though Delina has not seen Him, she loves Him; and even though Delina does not see Him now, she believes in Him and is filled with an inexpressible and glorious joy, for Delina is receiving the end result of her faith, the salvation of her soul.

1 Peter 1:8-9

Love

Delina loves the Lord with all of her heart, and with all of her soul, and with all of her strength.

Deuteronomy 6:5

Delina's love prospers; she is forgiving. Delina never dwells on a fault because it can separate close friends.

Proverbs 17:9

May Delina have power, together with all of the Lord's holy people, to grasp how wide and long and high and deep is the love of Christ.

Ephesians 3:18

And this is my prayer: that Delina's love may abound more and more in knowledge and depth of insight, so that Delina may be able to discern what is best and may be pure and blameless for the day of Christ.

Philippians 1:9-10

Obedience

As Delina listens to these commands of the Lord, and is careful to obey them, the Lord will make Delina the head and not the tail, and Delina will always be at the top and never at the bottom.

Deuteronomy 28:13

Delina walks in obedience to all that the Lord her God has commanded her, so that she may live and prosper and prolong her days in the land that she will possess.

Deuteronomy 5:33

Delina seeks You with all her heart; Delina will not stray from Your commands; Delina has hidden Your word in her heart that she may not sin against You.

Psalm 119:10-11

Obedience

Delina does not walk in the counsel of the ungodly or stand in the path of sinners or sit in the seat of scoffers. But Delina delights herself in the law of the Lord and Delina meditates on His law day and night. Delina is like a tree planted by the rivers of water, which yields its fruit in season and whose leaf will not wither, and whatever she does she prospers.

Psalm 1:1-3

Delina obeys her parents in the Lord. Delina honors her father and mother so that it may go well with her and that Delina may enjoy long life on earth.

Ephesians 6:1-3

Delina is a doer of the word, not a hearer only, deceiving herself.

James 1:22

Peace

Great peace has Delina, who loves Your law, and nothing can make her stumble.

Psalm 119:165

Delina is kept in perfect peace. Delina's mind is steadfast, because she trusts in You.

Isaiah 26:3

Great is the peace of Delina, for she is taught by the Lord.

Isaiah 54:13

Delina will go out in joy and be led forth in peace; the mountains and hills will burst into song before her, and all the trees of the field will clap their hands.

Isaiah 55:12

Peace

Jesus left Delina with a gift: peace of mind and heart. And the peace Jesus gave isn't like the peace the world gives. So Delina is not troubled or afraid.

John 14:27

Delina is not anxious about anything, but in everything by prayer and supplication with thanksgiving she lets her requests be made known to God. And the peace of God, which surpasses all understanding, guards Delina's heart and mind in Christ Jesus.

Philippians 4:6-7

Perseverance

Delina will not be overcome by evil circumstances. Delina will be long remembered. Delina does not fear bad news; she confidently trusts the Lord to care for her.

Psalm 112:6-7

Delina rejoices in her sufferings, because she knows that suffering produces perseverance, perseverance produces character, and character hope, and hope does not disappoint us.

Romans 5:3-4

Delina knows that in all things God works for the good of those who love Him, and have been called according to His purpose.

Romans 8:28

Perseverance

Forgetting what is behind, and straining toward what is ahead, Delina presses on towards the goal to win the prize for which God has called her heavenward in Christ Jesus.

Philippians 3:13-14

Delina rejoices always, prays continually, and gives thanks in all circumstances; for this is God's will for Delina in Christ Jesus.

1 Thessalonians 5:16-18

Delina never tires of doing what is good.

2 Thessalonians 3:13

Delina does not throw away her confident trust in the Lord. Delina is richly rewarded. Delina patiently endures, so that she will continue to do God's will. Then Delina will receive all that she has been promised.

Hebrews 10:35-36

Perseverance

Delina counts it all joy, my brothers, when she meets trials of various kinds, for she knows that the testing of her faith produces steadfastness. Delina lets steadfastness have its full effect, so that she may be perfect and complete, lacking in nothing.

James 1:2-4

Perseverance is finishing its work in Delina. Delina is mature and complete in Christ, not lacking anything. Delina asks God for wisdom and God gives Delina wisdom generously without finding fault.

James 1:4-5

In this Delina greatly rejoices, though now for a little while she may have had to suffer grief in all kinds of trials. These have come so that the proven genuineness of her faith—of greater worth than gold, which perishes even though refined by fire—may result in praise, glory, and honor when Jesus Christ is revealed.

1 Peter 1:6-7

Prayer

Delina prayed for her child, and the Lord has granted her what she asked of Him.

1 Samuel 1:27

Delina cries out, and the Lord hears, and delivers her out of her troubles.

Psalm 34:17

Delina calls upon God, and the Lord saves her. Evening, morning, and at noon, Delina will pray and cry aloud, and God hears her voice. God has redeemed Delina's soul in peace from the battle waged against her.

Psalm 55:16-18

And this is the confidence that Delina has toward Him, that if she asks anything according to His will He hears her.

1 John 5:14

Prayer

The Spirit helps Delina in weakness; for although Delina may not know how she should pray, the Spirit Himself intercedes for Delina with groanings too deep for words; and he who searches the hearts knows what the mind of the Spirit is, because He intercedes for Delina according to the will of God.

Romans 8:26-27

Delina rejoices always, prays without ceasing, gives thanks in all circumstances; for this is the will of God in Christ Jesus for her.

1 Thessalonians 5:16-18

With confidence Delina draws near to the throne of grace, that she may receive mercy and find grace to help her in time of need.

Hebrews 4:16

Delina casts all her anxiety on God because He cares for Delina.

1 Peter 5:7

Promise

Delina has been trained up in the way she should go; and when she is old, she will not depart from it.

Proverbs 22:6

"And I will give Delina a new heart, and a new spirit I will put within her. And I will remove the heart of stone from Delina's flesh and give her a heart of flesh. And I will put my spirit within Delina, and cause her to walk in my statutes and she will be careful to obey my rules."

Ezekiel 36:26-27

He who began a good work in Delina will be faithful to complete it.

Philippians 1:6

As Delina draws near to God, God draws near to Delina.

James 4:8

Provision

The Lord is Delina's shepherd; Delina lacks nothing.

Psalm 23:1

The lions may grow weak and hungry, but Delina seeks the Lord and lacks no good thing.

Psalm 34:10

For the Lord God is Delina's sun and shield; the Lord bestows favor and honor on Delina; no good thing does He withhold from Delina whose walk is blameless.

Psalm 84:11

The Lord will guide Delina always; He will satisfy Delina's needs in a sun-scorched land and will strengthen Delina's frame. Delina will be like a well-watered garden, like a spring whose waters never fail.

Isaiah 58:11

Provision

And God is able to make all grace abound to Delina, so that in all things at all times, Delina has all that she needs; Delina will abound in every good work.

2 Corinthians 9:8

And my God will meet all of Delina's needs according to the riches of His glory, Christ Jesus.

Philippians 4:19

His divine power has given Delina everything she needs for life and godliness through her knowledge of Him who called Delina by His own glory and goodness.

2 Peter 1:3

Purity

Create in Delina a clean heart, O God, and renew a right spirit within her.

Psalm 51:10

Blessed is Delina, who is pure in heart, for she will see God.

Matthew 5:8

If Delina confesses her sins, He is faithful and just to forgive her sins, and to cleanse Delina from all unrighteousness.

1 John 1:9

Purity

Grace and peace be multiplied unto Delina through the knowledge of God, and of Jesus our Lord. His divine power has granted to Delina all things that pertain to life and godliness, through the knowledge of Him who called Delina to His glory and excellence, by which He has granted to her His precious and very great promises, so that through them Delina may become a partaker of the divine nature, having escaped from the corruption that is in the world because of sinful desire.

2 Peter 1:1-4

Redemption

Delina calls upon God, and the Lord saves her. Evening, morning, and at noon, Delina will pray and cry aloud, and God hears her voice. God has redeemed Delina's soul in peace from the battle waged against her.

Psalm 55:16-18

Do not gloat over Delina, enemy! Though Delina has fallen, she will rise; though Delina sits in darkness, the Lord will be her light. Because she has sinned against Him, she will bear the consequences, until He pleads Delina's case and establishes her right. He will bring Delina into the light and Delina will see His righteousness.

Micah 7:8-9

Delina has been crucified with Christ. Delina no longer lives, but Christ lives in her. The life Delina now lives in the body, she lives by faith in the Son of God, who loved her and gave Himself for her.

Galatians 2:20

Revelation

Do not gloat over Delina, enemy! Though Delina has fallen, she will rise; though Delina sits in darkness, the Lord will be her light. Because she has sinned against Him, she will bear the consequences, until He pleads Delina's case and establishes her right. He will bring Delina into the light and Delina will see His righteousness.

Micah 7:8-9

What Delina has received is not the spirit of the world, but the Spirit who is from God, so that she may understand what God has freely given her.

1 Corinthians 2:12

Delina has the mind of Christ and the wisdom of God is formed within her.

1 Corinthians 2:16

Revelation

God, bring to light and remove any darkness in Delina's heart. He will expose any wrong motives to her.

1 Corinthians 4:5

Whenever Delina turns to the Lord, the veil is taken away.

2 Corinthians 3:16

May the Lord Jesus Christ give Delina the Spirit of wisdom and of revelation in the knowledge of Him, having the eyes of her heart enlightened, that Delina may know what is the hope to which He has called her, what are the riches of his glorious inheritance in the saints, and what is the immeasurable greatness of His power toward us who believe, according to the working of His great might.

Ephesians 1:17-19

Righteousness

The Lord dealt with Delina according to her righteousness; according to the cleanness of her hands He rewarded her.

2 Samuel 22:21

Delina clothes herself with the Lord Jesus Christ, and does not think about how to gratify the desires of the flesh.

Romans 13:14

He who supplies seed to the sower and bread for food will supply and multiply Delina's seed for sowing and increase the harvest of her righteousness.

2 Corinthians 9:10

Delina is filled with the fruit of righteousness that comes through Jesus Christ, to the glory and praise of God.

Philippians 1:11

Righteousness

Delina flees the evil desires of her youth and pursues righteousness, faith, love, and peace, along with those who call on the Lord out of a pure heart.

2 Timothy 2:22

Safety & Protection

God is Delina's rock, in whom she takes refuge, her shield and the horn of her salvation. He is Delina's stronghold, her refuge and her savior—from violent people Delina is saved. She calls to the Lord, who is worthy of praise, and Delina is saved from her enemies.

2 Samuel 22:3-4

Delina is safe and hidden in the Lord's shadow away from danger.

Psalm 91:1

Do not withhold Your mercy from Delina, O Lord; may Your love and Your truth always protect her.

Psalm 40:11

The Lord's angels keep charge over Delina to guard her in all her ways.

Psalm 91:11

Safety & Protection

Delina's integrity and uprightness protect her, because Delina's hope, Lord, is in You.

Psalm 25:21

Delina has made the Most High her dwelling place. No harm will befall Delina; no disaster will come near her tent. For He will give His angels charge over Delina to guard her in all of her ways. They will carry her so that Delina does not dash her foot against a stone. They will tread upon the lion and the cobra; they will trample them underfoot. Because Delina loves You, You will deliver her. You will set Delina on high. Delina will call upon You and You will answer her. You will be with Delina in trouble. You will deliver Delina and honor her with a long life. You will satisfy Delina and show her Your salvation.

Psalm 91:9-16

Safety & Protection

When Delina lies down, she will not be afraid; when Delina lies down, her sleep will be sweet. Delina has no fear of sudden disaster or of the ruin that overtakes the wicked, for the Lord is at her side and will keep her foot from being snared.

Proverbs 3:24-26

Delina is taught by the Lord and great will be Delina's peace, her health, safety, protection, and prosperity. In righteousness Delina will be established. Tyranny will be far from Delina; Delina will have nothing to fear. Terror will be far removed; it will not come near Delina. No weapon forged against Delina will prosper.

Isaiah 54:13-14, 17

Delina is afflicted in every way, but not crushed; perplexed, but not driven to despair; persecuted, but not forsaken; struck down, but not destroyed.

2 Corinthians 4:8-9

Salvation

Delina calls upon God, and the Lord saves her. Evening, morning, and at noon, Delina will pray and cry aloud, and God hears her voice. God has redeemed Delina's soul in peace from the battle waged against her.

Psalm 55:16-18

I am convinced that neither death nor life, neither angels nor demons, neither the present nor the future, nor any powers, neither height nor depth, nor anything else in all creation, will be able to separate Delina from the love of God that is in Christ Jesus our Lord.

Romans 8:38-39

Delina confesses with her mouth that Jesus is Lord and Delina believes in her heart that You have raised Christ from the dead. Delina calls on Your name, Lord! Delina is saved as one of Your children.

Romans 10:9-13

Salvation

Delina finds her salvation in repentance and rest. Delina's strength is in quietness and trust.

Isaiah 30:15

Praise be to the God and Father of our Lord Jesus Christ! In His great mercy He has given Delina new birth into a living hope through the resurrection of Jesus Christ from the dead, and into an inheritance that can never perish, spoil, or fade. This inheritance is kept in heaven for Delina, who through faith is shielded by God's power until the coming of the salvation that is ready to be revealed in the last time.

1 Peter 1:3-4

Though Delina has not seen Him, she loves Him; and even though Delina does not see Him now, she believes in Him and is filled with an inexpressible and glorious joy, for Delina is receiving the end result of her faith, the salvation of her soul.

1 Peter 1:8-9

Seeking God

Delina will seek the Lord her God and she will find Him, if she searches after Him with all her heart and with all her soul.

Deuteronomy 4:29

Deal bountifully with Delina, that she may live and keep Your word. Open Delina's eyes that she may behold wondrous things out of the word.

Psalm 119:17-18

O God, You are Delina's God, earnestly she seeks You; Delina's soul thirsts for You, her body longs for You in a dry and weary land where there is no water. Delina has seen You in the sanctuary and beheld Your power and Your glory. Because Your love is better than life, Delina's lips will glorify You.

Psalm 63:1-3

Seeking God

"I love Delina who loves me, and as Delina seeks me so she will find me."

Proverbs 8:17

"Delina will call upon me and come and pray to me, and I will hear her. Delina will seek me and find me, when she seeks me with all her heart. I will be found by Delina," declares the Lord.

Jeremiah 20:12-14

The Lord is good to Delina whose hope is in Him, to Delina who seeks Him.

Lamentations 3:25

Delina has the mind of Christ and the wisdom of God is formed within her.

1 Corinthians 2:16

Seeking God

Forgetting what is behind, and straining toward what is ahead, Delina presses on towards the goal to win the prize for which God has called her heavenward in Christ Jesus.

Philippians 3:13-14

Delina draws near to God, and He draws near to her.

James 4:8

Spiritual Growth

He who supplies seed to the sower and bread for food will supply and multiply Delina's seed for sowing and increase the harvest of her righteousness.

2 Corinthians 9:10

Delina, speaking the truth in love, grows up in every way into Him who is the head, into Christ.

Ephesians 4:15

Delina walks in a manner worthy of the Lord, fully pleasing Him, bearing fruit in every good work and growing in the knowledge of God. Delina is strengthened with all power according to His glorious might so that she has great endurance and patience.

Colossians 1:10-11

Delina leaves the elementary doctrine of Christ and goes on to maturity, not laying again the foundation of repentance from dead works and of faith in God.

Hebrews 6:1

Spiritual Growth

Delina is growing in the grace and knowledge of our Lord and savior Jesus Christ. To Him be glory both now and forever! Amen.

2 Peter 3:18

Spiritual Warfare

Delina is strong in the Lord and in His mighty power. Delina puts on the full armor of God, so that she can take her stand against the devil's schemes. For Delina's struggles are not against flesh and blood, but against the rulers, against the authorities, against the powers of this dark world and against the spiritual forces of evil in the heavenly realms. Therefore, Delina puts on the full armor of God, so that when the day of evil comes, Delina will stand her ground. Delina stands firm with the belt of truth buckled around her waist, with the breastplate of righteousness in place, and with her feet fitted with the readiness that comes from the gospel of peace. In addition to all this, Delina takes up the shield of faith, with which she can extinguish all the flaming arrows of the evil one. Delina takes the helmet of salvation and the sword of the Spirit, which is the word of God.

Ephesians 6:10-17

Spiritual Warfare

Delina calls upon God, and the Lord saves her. Evening, morning, and at noon, Delina will pray and cry aloud, and God hears her voice. God has redeemed Delina's soul in peace from the battle waged against her.

Psalm 55:16-18

Delina has authority to trample on snakes and scorpions and to overcome all the power of the enemy; nothing will harm Delina.

Luke 10:19

In all things Delina is more than a conqueror through Him who loved us. For I am convinced that neither death nor life, neither angels nor demons, neither the present nor future, nor any powers, neither height nor depth, nor anything else in all creation, will be able to separate Delina from the love of God that is in Christ Jesus our Lord.

Romans 8:37-39

Spiritual Warfare

Delina is not overcome by evil, but Delina overcomes evil with good.

Romans 12:21

No temptation has overtaken Delina except what is common to mankind. And God is faithful; He will not let Delina be tempted beyond what she can bear. But when Delina is tempted, He will also provide a way out so that she can endure it.

1 Corinthians 10:13

Delina demolishes arguments and every pretension that sets itself up against the knowledge of God, and Delina takes captive every thought and makes it obedient to Christ.

2 Corinthians 10:5

Spiritual Warfare

Delina is delivered from the evils of this present world, for it is the will of God.

Galatians 1:4

Delina is an overcomer and Delina overcomes by the blood of the Lamb and the word of her testimony.

Revelation 12:11

Strength

It is God who arms Delina with strength and makes her way perfect. God makes Delina's feet like the feet of a deer; He enables Delina to stand on the heights.

2 Samuel 22:33-34

The joy of the Lord is Delina's strength. The Lord is the strength of Delina's life.

Nehemiah 8:10

Create in Delina a pure heart, O God, and renew a steadfast spirit within her. Restore to Delina the joy of Your salvation and grant her a willing spirit, to sustain her.

Psalm 51:10,12

Strength

Delina does not walk in the counsel of the ungodly or stand in the path of sinners or sit in the seat of scoffers. But Delina delights herself in the law of the Lord and Delina meditates on His law day and night. Delina is like a tree planted by the rivers of water, which yields its fruit in season and whose leaf will not wither, and whatever she does she prospers.

Psalm 1:1-3

Delina will never be shaken; Delina will be remembered forever. Delina will not fear bad news; her heart is steadfast, trusting in the Lord. Delina's heart is upheld, she will not fear.

Psalm 112:6-8

The Lord makes firm the steps of Delina who delights in him; though Delina stumbles, she will not fall, for the Lord upholds her with His hand.

Psalm 37:23-24

Strength

Delina finds her salvation in repentance and rest. Delina's strength is in quietness and trust.

Isaiah 30:15

Delina hopes in the Lord and the Lord renews her strength. Delina will soar on wings like an eagle. Delina will run and not grow weary. Delina will walk and not be faint.

Isaiah 40:31

Greater is He who is in Delina, than he who is in the world.

1 John 4:4

Delina receives the gift of the Holy Spirit. Delina receives power when the Holy Spirit comes upon her.

Acts 2:38, 1:8

Strength

Delina can do all things through Christ who strengthens her.

Philippians 4:13

Delina walks in a manner worthy of the Lord, fully pleasing Him, bearing fruit in every good work and growing in the knowledge of God. Delina is strengthened with all power according to His glorious might so that she has great endurance and patience.

Colossians 1:10-11

Just as Delina received Christ Jesus as Lord, she continues to live in Him. Delina is rooted and built up in Him, strengthened in faith as she was taught, and overflowing with thankfulness.

Colossians 2:6-7

The Lord is faithful, and He will strengthen Delina and protect her from the evil one.

2 Thessalonians 3:3

Transformation

Delina delights herself in the Lord and the Lord gives Delina the desires of her heart.

Psalm 37:4

Delina is not conformed to the pattern of this world but she is transformed by the renewing of her mind. Delina's mind is renewed by the word of God.

Romans 12:2

Delina is a new creation in Christ Jesus.

2 Corinthians 5:17

Delina does not lose heart. Though outwardly she is wasting away, yet inwardly Delina is being renewed day by day, for Delina's light and momentary troubles are achieving for her an eternal glory that far outweighs them all. So Delina fixes her eyes not on what is seen, but what is unseen, since what is seen is temporary, but what is unseen is eternal.

2 Corinthians 4:16-18

Transformation

Delina has been crucified with Christ. Delina no longer lives, but Christ lives in her. The life Delina now lives in the body, she lives by faith in the Son of God, who loved her and gave Himself for her.

Galatians 2:20

He who began a good work in Delina will be faithful to complete it.

Philippians 1:6

May God Himself, the God of peace, sanctify Delina through and through. May Delina's whole spirit, soul, and body be kept blameless at the coming of our Lord Jesus Christ.

1 Thessalonians 5:23

Trials

Indeed, Delina felt that she had received the sentence of death. But that was to make her rely not on herself but on God, who raises the dead.

2 Corinthians 1:9

In all this you greatly rejoice, though now for a little while Delina may have had to suffer grief in all kinds of trials. These have come so that the proven genuineness of Delina's faith—of greater worth than gold, which perishes even though refined by fire—may result in praise, glory, and honor when Jesus Christ is revealed.

1 Peter 1:6-7

And the God of all grace, who called Delina to His eternal glory in Christ, after Delina has suffered a little while, will Himself restore her and make her strong, firm and steadfast.

1 Peter 5:10

Trust

Some trust in chariots and some in horses, but Delina trusts in the name of the Lord our God.

Psalm 20:7

Delina trusts in the Lord with all her heart, and does not lean on her own understanding. In all Delina's ways she acknowledges Him, and He will direct her path.

Proverbs 3:5-6

Delina does not throw away her confident trust in the Lord. Delina is richly rewarded. Delina has patient endurance so that she continues to do God's will. Then Delina will receive all that she has been promised.

Hebrews 10:35-36

Wisdom

The Spirit of the Lord will rest on Delina—the Spirit of wisdom and of understanding, the Spirit of counsel and of might, the Spirit of the knowledge and fear of the Lord.

Isaiah 11:2

I keep asking that the God of our Lord Jesus Christ, the glorious Father, may give Delina the Spirit of wisdom and revelation, so that she may know Him better. I pray that the eyes of Delina's heart may be enlightened in order that she may know the hope to which He has called her, the riches of His glorious inheritance in His holy people, and His incomparably great power for us who believe.

Ephesians 1:17-19

And this is my prayer: that Delina's love may abound more and more in knowledge and depth of insight, so that Delina may be able to discern what is best and may be pure and blameless for the day of Christ. May Delina be filled with the fruit of righteousness that comes through Jesus Christ to the glory and praise of God.

Philippians 1:9-11

Wisdom

Delina is filled with the knowledge of the Lord's will and all wisdom and spiritual understanding.

Colossians 1:9

When Delina lacks wisdom, she asks God who gives generously to all without finding fault, and it will be given to her.

James 1:5

Worship

Delina trusts in Your unfailing love; her heart rejoices in Your salvation. Delina sings to the Lord, for He has been good to her.

Psalm 13:5-6

In view of God's mercy, Delina offers her body as a living sacrifice, holy and pleasing to God—this is her spiritual act of worship.

Romans 12:1

Delina is grateful for receiving a kingdom that cannot be shaken, and she offers to God acceptable worship, with reverence and awe, for our God is a consuming fire.

Hebrews 12:28-29

Delina fears God and gives Him glory, because the hour of His judgment has come. Delina worships Him who made the heavens, the earth, the sea and the springs of water.

Revelation 14:7

AUTHOR'S NOTE

Biblical reference Hebrews 4:12 says that God's word is alive and powerful, sharper than a two-edged sword. When we speak and pray the Scriptures, we are coming into agreement with God, and His power is released to answer our prayers; and by doing so we strengthen the expression of our prayer. As we pray the word of God we will learn who He is, and who He has made us to be. When we are living in the fullness of our true identity in Christ, we will then experience God and all He has intended for us.

TESTIMONY

It never occurred to me that I would write a book. This was not a secret dream or desire. It was in a desperate moment of brokenness and confusion that the Holy Spirit led me to write my first book of prayers for my husband Peter and I. I was in a season of many tears, anxiety, and barely any sleep. To say I was lost is an understatement! All I knew was that I was a woman committed to her marriage through God, and yet I found myself separated from my husband after being divorced and remarried... again.

I felt regret, failure, fear, exhaustion, and sadness. Somehow, having been in this situation before didn't help any. In fact it made me feel worse. My prayer life was barely alive because I found myself in such a pathetic state. Sometimes all I could pray was "I trust You, Lord." Being so empty, this statement was all I had to offer. I was so messed up that it felt like I said it every thirty seconds.

I entered into a season in which the Lord told me not to talk to my husband. All of our conversations were leading to more division. The only way God allowed me to contact Peter was by sending him loving or encouraging text messages and scriptures. He also led me to start writing scriptures down and inserting our names into them. Although still broken, my prayers were empowered. I was praying God's will for our lives. I was unleashing the power of the Holy Spirit into my marriage. I wrote these scriptures on little white spiral-bound note cards. This task sustained me through a terrible time, transformed both of our hearts, and I believe it brought my husband and I back together.

I understand that not all trials end in victory. Because Peter and I are human, we will have struggles again. But I will never stop using the gift that God gave me. It changes me continually. And during the time I described above the prayers enabled me to function as a mom in an upside-down world.

I soon realized the power these little books had and started writing them for my children and for the people around me who were going through tough times. The response was unbelievable. I heard things like "This is just what I needed," and many stories of hope and change.

If you are looking to grow in your relationship with God or to overcome a difficult situation, I encourage you to pray this little book and to pray it for those you love. Get ready to be transformed and to be a world changer. Life will never be the same.

ABOUT THE AUTHOR

Michelle Leslie was raised in rural Oregon. She is a pillar of activation within the Body of Christ with a heart to hear God's word and see it lived out as her calling and destiny. Along with her gift for challenging people to be all they were created to be in their life, she is a fun-loving, hard-working, creative friend, daughter, mom, and wife.

As a child, Michelle was dyslexic. Because of her trouble learning to read, she struggled through every subject in school and was doomed to special education classes (which she perceived as "social suicide"). When Michelle came to know the Lord in her early twenties she was desperate for God's word. As she dove into the word of God, her life changed dramatically. Romans 12:2 was in full effect, and Michelle was transformed by the renewing of her mind. The effects of the learning disability that had held Michelle back her whole life were slowly diminishing. Michelle was finally reading and retaining information, growing in confidence, and developing a voice for the message God had given her to share. God's power was being made perfect in her weakness, and through this platform God demonstrated his love and transforming power to those around her.

Michelle has a deep desire for others to experience the transformation and freedom that can only be found in Christ, and she is sharing it with all who will listen through this extraordinary upcoming book, *Activating God's Power.*

Michelle is writing in the hope of meeting the needs of readers in desperation, or those who are seeking spiritual growth in themselves or in their loved ones. Michelle lives in Denver, Colorado with her husband and two daughters.

CONTACT

To order books please see instructions at:
www.MichelleLeslie.net

To contact Michelle Leslie directly:
Michelle@MichelleLeslie.net

Follow Michelle Leslie online:

Facebook.com/MichelleLeslie.net

@MichelleLeslie_

MichelleLeslie_

CPSIA information can be obtained
at www.ICGtesting.com
Printed in the USA
BVHW041028140523
664128BV00004B/76